BEAR MARKET TRADING STRATEGIES

MATTHEW R. KRATTER

WWW.TRADER.UNIVERSITY

CONTENTS

Disclaimer	vii
Your Free Gift	ix
1. Introduction	1
2. How to Spot a Bear Market on the Horizon	9
3. Bear Market Trading Strategies That Actually Work	20
4. An Automated Trading Strategy That Makes Big Money in a Bear Market	32
5. How to Tell When a Bear Market is Almost Over	38
6. How to Short Momentum Stocks in a Bear Market	45
7. What Stocks to Buy When Everyone Else is Selling	57
Also By Matthew R. Kratter	65
Your Free Gift	67
About the Author	69
Disclaimer	71

Copyright © 2018 by Little Cash Machines LLC

All rights reserved. No part of this book may be reproduced in any form without written permission from the author (matt@trader.university). Reviewers may quote brief passages in reviews.

For my children

DISCLAIMER

Neither Little Cash Machines LLC, nor any of its directors, officers, shareholders, personnel, representatives, agents, or independent contractors (collectively, the "Operator Parties") are licensed financial advisers, registered investment advisers, or registered broker-dealers. None of the Operator Parties are providing investment, financial, legal, or tax advice, and nothing in this book or at www.Trader.University (henceforth, "the Site") should be construed as such by you. This book and the Site should be used as educational tools only and are not replacements for professional investment advice. The full disclaimer can be found at the end of this book.

YOUR FREE GIFT

Thanks for buying my book!

As a way of showing my appreciation, I've created a **Free Video Tutorial** for you.

In this video, I am going to show you some of the tools and charts that I use in my trading.

I will also give you an exact copy of the trading chart that I use to track bull and bear markets.

There was no way to include this material in a written book, so I have created this free video tutorial for you instead.

>>>Tap Here to Get the Free Video Tutorial and Charts<<<

Or simply go to:

http://www.trader.university/bear-market

ONE
INTRODUCTION

If you spend enough time in the markets, there is a 100% chance that you will experience a bear market in your lifetime.

And probably multiple bear markets.

If you've already lived through one, you know how difficult they can be.

If you've never experienced a bear market, there is a good chance that you are not prepared for one.

Warren Buffett is famous for saying:

> "Only when the tide goes out do you discover who's been swimming naked."

A bull market lifts all boats.

If you make trading mistakes, the gradually rising tide will usually bail you out.

Not so in a bear market.

When the tide rushes out, you can spot the newbie traders and fraudsters lying on the sand.

I don't want this to happen to you.

I want you to be prepared for the next bear market.

I've lived through the great bear markets of 2000-2002 and 2008-2009.

In each one, I made some mistakes, but ultimately emerged wealthier (and wiser).

I want to share with you what I've learned.

This book will give you all the tools that you'll need to spot a bear market on the horizon—and then to profit from it.

Here's how I define bull and bear markets.

A bull market looks like this:

In a bull market, a stock market index (a collection of stocks, like the S&P 500) spends most of its time trading above the 50-day moving average (the top blue line in the image).

And the 50-day moving average is above the 200-day moving average (the lower red line in the image).

The chart begins on the lower left-hand side of the page and finishes at the top right-hand side of the page.

That's a bull market.

A bear market looks like this:

In a bear market, a stock market index spends most of its time below the 50-day moving average (the lower blue line in the image).

And the 50-day moving average is trading below the 200-day moving average (the upper red line in the image).

The chart begins on the upper left-hand side of the page and finishes in the lower right-hand side of the page.

Bull markets are almost always a leisurely affair.

They take their time to develop, and usually last 5-15 years.

Bull markets last until everyone is comfortable.

Bull markets make sure that almost everyone is fully invested—and even using lots of margin (borrowed money).

Bull markets last long enough to make sure that all of the amateurs feel like stock market geniuses.

Bull markets feel like a leisurely 10-course meal.

A smooth steady push upwards.

Not so with bear markets.

If bull markets take the escalator up, then bear markets take the elevator shaft down.

Bear markets are fast and furious.

They usually last 6 months to 2.5 years.

Bear markets feel like a crack in the earth opening up and swallowing you.

In a bull market, volatility (how much the market bounces around) usually stays low.

If the market dips (sells off a bit), everyone jumps in to "buy the dip."

This happens again and again, until a whole generation has been trained to always buy the dip.

When everyone buys every dip, it helps to keep volatility low.

Today everyone is talking about "BTFD"—"buy the f***ing dip."

We live in vulgar times, but the principle is the same.

Buying the dip has worked extremely well since 2009, but is about to end.

A dip is coming that is going to take out a whole generation.

In a bear market, traders who buy the dip get crushed.

As soon as they've loaded up on their position, the bottom falls out.

In a panic, they exit their positions and try to get short (betting on a continued market decline).

As soon as they are short, a fast and furious rally arrives and blows them out of their short position.

In a bear market, there are plunges followed by 2-5 day melt-ups.

Volatility is high.

You are glued to your computer screen and news feed.

Your cortisol levels and other stress hormones stay high.

Your neck and lower back ache all the time.

You see numbers on your screen and cannot believe your eyes.

Companies file for bankruptcy.

Some stocks go to zero.

You might even own a few of them.

In a bear market, you feel like you are walking in a dream.

The feeling is similar to the death of a loved one.

Disbelief, numbness, grief.

There's only one way to stay sane:

Know what to expect in advance.

In the next chapter, I will give you the road map, so that you will recognize signposts on the journey.

TWO

HOW TO SPOT A BEAR MARKET ON THE HORIZON

After the stock market has been going up for many years, you will reach a point where you feel like you are missing out.

All of your friends and neighbors will be bragging about how much money they are making.

Your wife will be asking you why you don't own stock XYZ.

You'll try to buy some more stocks, but will find that they are getting away from you.

You had a chance to buy that stock at 70 last month.

Yesterday it was at 90.

Today it's at 110 after reporting great earnings.

You're tired of waiting for a pullback that never comes.

So you take that chunk of cash (that you've been holding for 5 years), and use it to buy some random stocks that everyone is talking about.

Chances are, you've never read a 10-K for those stocks, or analyzed their charts.

But you feel good that you are going to finally make some money with everyone else.

For a few days, you are coining money.

The stocks that you have bought keep moving up.

Like little toy soldiers, they are steadily marching upwards.

Volatility is low, and every dip in the stock gets bought.

Suddenly you wake up one Monday morning and the Dow is down 400 points.

You look at your account and can't believe your eyes.

Some of your stocks are down 3% and a few are even down 8%.

High volatility has returned to the markets.

The steady climb upwards is over.

Now you get to watch your stocks bounce all over the place.

You're sweating bullets for a few days, but fortunately your stocks recover.

You're almost back to your entry points in all of them.

One Friday afternoon, all of your stocks are up 3-5% on the day, and you're feeling like a genius again.

The pundits on TV have all declared that the correction is over.

There's still lots of volatility, but at least stocks are moving up.

Unfortunately, none of your stocks seem to be able to make it back up to their highs.

They keep bouncing around within a range (say from 90 to 110).

In addition, the SPY (S&P 500) and QQQ (NASDAQ 100) are having trouble staying above their 50-day moving averages for more than a few days.

Each 50-day moving average begins to droop and turn down.

During the bull market, they were pointing northeast on the chart.

Now they're pointing southeast on the chart.

Then one bleak day, you realize that the 50-day moving average for the SPY has just moved below the 200-day moving average.

Then the roller coaster begins.

The markets close lower every day for 10 days.

Everyone keeps saying how oversold the market is, but this time there is no bounce.

Traders who bought the dip 5 days ago are now down 10% and sick to their stomachs.

The 50-day moving average is in a race to the bottom with the 200-day moving average.

The VIX (volatility index) is now firmly above 20 and shows no sign of coming down.

At some point, the SPY or QQQ may begin to trade above the 50-day moving average.

Don't be fooled.

As long as the 50-day moving average is far below the 200-day moving average, this is probably a fake rally.

In a bear market, lots of smart traders will try to short the market.

They will borrow shares of a stock, sell them on the market, and then try to buy them back a lower price.

When you buy a stock, you try to buy low and sell high.

When you short a stock, you try to sell high and buy low.

When you short a stock and it moves up, you lose money.

If it moves up quickly, you lose money quickly.

You then have to try to buy back your shares as quickly as possible.

Even in a bear market, this buying pressure can make a stock move up quickly, as the shorts try to exit their positions.

This is why you can sometimes see days in a bear market where the markets are up a lot.

The Dow might be up 500 points.

Don't be deceived, especially if the market has only been selling off for a few months.

And especially if the 50-day moving average for the SPY or QQQ is still below the 200-day moving average.

A true bear market takes 6 months to 2.5 years to unfold.

Quick short-covering rallies will quickly exhaust themselves, and then the markets will once again turn south.

Here's one trading strategy that you can use to profit from this short-covering.

First, you MUST have in place the following conditions:

- The stock market must have been going up for the past 5-10 years.
- Then the 50-day moving average for the SPY must have moved below the 200-day moving average and stayed there for at least 4 months.
- The 50-day moving average for the SPY must still be below the 200-day moving average.

If these three conditions are true, and the SPY trades above the 200-day moving average, you can short the SPY (or S&P E-mini futures) anywhere above the 200-day moving average line.

The SPY should begin to sell off within a day or two.

If it does not, you know you are wrong and should exit your position immediately.

Exit your position for a profit when the SPY closes below the 50-day moving average.

If you are an aggressive trader, you might be able to hold on to this short for an additional few weeks (or even months) to milk it for even more profit.

Here is what this trade looked like on 19 May 2008:

The SPY traded above the 200-day moving average intraday, but failed to close at those levels.

You can see from the long upper "wick" of the candlestick that the SPY was unable to hold those levels intraday.

It is not a coincidence that this short-covering rally failed right at the 200-day moving average line.

That is a key level that is watched by many market participants.

When it fails to hold, it can become a self-fulfilling prophecy.

In fact, you can see that the SPY continued to fall until mid July.

This is the best way to profit from a short-covering rally in a bear market.

Never try to short the market after it has been selling off for multiple days.

Much better to wait for the end of an exhaustion rally as we've seen in this example.

A good entry point will give you immediate profits.

And these profits will make it much more comfortable to hold the position as a swing-trade.

If you are super aggressive and doing this trade with futures, you can even use your open profits as initial margin to sell more futures contracts.

This is called "pyramiding" from the short side, and is an extremely advanced trading strategy.

This "failure at the 200-day moving average" trade worked well during the 2000-2002 bear market as well.

Here is a good example from 4 January 2002:

And another good example from 4 March 2002:

In the latter example, we were already about 1.5 years into the bear market, which made the trade a bit more dangerous.

You can see how the SPY spent more time than usual above the 200-day moving average before plunging once more.

For this reason, it is best to use this trade 4 months to 1 year into a bear market.

In the next chapter, we will look at another way to profit from a bear market.

THREE
BEAR MARKET TRADING STRATEGIES THAT ACTUALLY WORK

We've discussed that a bear market begins only when a long bull market comes to an end.

For major indices like SPY and QQQ, the 50-day moving average crosses below the 200-day moving average.

And then stays there for 6 months to over 2 years.

Over this period of time, stocks can go down a lot.

During the bear market of 2000-2002, many internet stocks went down 85-95% from their highs.

And more than a few went to zero.

At the same time, the S&P 500 went down 49% and the Dow went down 38%.

I'm always getting emails from my readers asking me how to profit from a bear market like this.

In this chapter, we will cover a few of the ways.

The biggest problem with trading bear markets is the "negative carry" involved.

Let me explain.

Normally when you hold stocks, you get paid.

You may get paid an actual dividend, or you may get paid "implicitly" by the fact that most stocks go up most of the time.

Getting paid while you hold a position is called "positive carry."

Each day you get paid a little bit.

That feels good.

What doesn't feel good is losing a little money every day.

That feels bad-- like death by multiple paper-cuts.

That's what "negative carry" is.

If you short stocks, you normally have to pay (rather than receive) the dividend.

You also have to pay a fee ("the borrow") to your broker in order to short the stock.

That's negative carry.

You lose a little money every day, so you have to time the trade perfectly in order to come out ahead.

If you buy puts on the stock market, you also have negative carry.

Because of time decay, your puts will lose a little bit of money every day.

That's another form of negative carry.

But it gets worse.

Put options are cheap only when volatility is low.

Volatility is only low during a bull market.

Once the market thinks that we might be in a bear market, the price of put options shoots up.

Buying puts in a bear market is little bit like buying flood insurance when your basement is already filling up with water.

Of course, buying puts in a **bull** market is like buying life insurance when you're young and healthy.

Who does that?

So we're in a bit of a quandary.

There are easier ways to make money, but if you are intent on buying puts, here is how I would do it.

Let's say that SPY is currently at 271, and I think that it is going to go down 40% over the next 12 months.

If SPY falls 40%, it will be trading at 162.60.

So then I go here and look at the put options for 15 March 2019 (one year from now):

https://finance.yahoo.com/quote/SPY/options?p=SPY

The 15 March 2019 SPY puts with a strike price of 170 are currently offered at 1.58.

If the SPY is trading at 162.60 on 15 March 2019, those options will be worth (170.00 minus 162.60 equals 7.40) right before expiration.

If my timing is perfect, I can buy the puts at 1.58 today and sell them for 7.40 next March.

If I invest $10,000 in this trade, it will make me $36,835 in profits.

You can adjust the strike price or expiration date to change the risk/reward ratio of the trade.

Remember that options lose most of their time value in the final 60 days going into option expiration.

If you choose to buy put options, only do it with money that you can afford to lose.

If you wait for the SPY or QQQ 50-day moving average to cross below the 200-day moving average, you will almost certainly have to pay more for the puts.

However, if you try to buy puts before this crossover occurs, there's a risk that your puts will decay a lot or even expire before the bear market actually gets underway.

This is always the dilemma behind negative carry trades.

Fortunately there is another bear market trading strategy that is currently positive carry (as of today 22 March 2018).

In other words, it implicitly pays you every day to hold the position.

As we have discussed, the S&P 500 is a collection of 500 stocks.

It is a good representation of what's currently going on in the U.S. stock market.

If you buy the SPY (an ETF that mirrors the S&P 500), you are buying little pieces of all of these stocks.

You can also trade futures on the S&P 500—they're called the S&P E-mini futures.

(I like to use TradeStation and Interactive Brokers for trading futures).

If you buy these futures, you are betting that the S&P 500 will go up.

If you sell these futures, you are betting that the S&P 500 will go down.

The nice thing about these futures is that they enable you to use leverage.

Yesterday, the June 2018 S&P 500 E-mini futures closed at 2718.

Each point on the futures contract is worth $50.

So to find the value of 1 S&P E-mini futures contract, you just multiply this 2718 by $50 to get $135,900.

That's the "notional value" of one E-mini futures contract.

Now the good news is that you can currently buy one of these futures contracts by putting up just $6,380.

In other words, you only have to put up 4.69% of the value, and you still get to control the whole futures contract.

That $6,380 is what's called "initial margin."

Put that much money into your futures trading account, and they will let you buy 1 E-mini futures contract.

If you buy 1 futures contract and the price moves up from 2718 to 2719, you make $50.

If you buy 1 futures contract and the price moves up from 2718 to 2818, you make $5,000 (100 points times $50/point).

That's a return of over 78%, since you only needed $6,380 in your account to make the trade.

Of course, if the price moves down 100 points instead, you'll lose $5,000.

If your initial margin falls from $6,380 to $5,800, your futures broker will make you add another $580 to your account in order to keep the position open.

That $5,800 is what's called "maintenance margin."

So leverage is a two-edged sword.

It can magnify both profits and losses.

Because futures use leverage they are not for anyone.

A conservative way to trade futures is to keep a lot more cash in your account than you need to.

So if initial margin is $6,380, just multiply that amount by 4 and keep $25,520 in your account for every 1 contract that you want to trade.

Your returns will be lower, but you will also sleep better at night.

So here's the trading system:

When the S&P 500 50-day moving average closes below the 200-day moving average, you sell 1 (or more) S&P 500 E-mini futures contract.

When the 50-day moving average moves back above the 200-day moving average, you exit your position by buying 1 futures contract.

If you have sold 1 futures contract, and then you buy 1 futures contract of the same kind, it will close the trade and effectively lock in your profit or loss.

I've created a chart here that you can use to monitor these moving crossovers:

https://www.tradingview.com/chart/WobeoiHE/

Let's see how this system worked during the last great bear market.

On 21 December 2007, the 50-day moving average closed below the 200-day moving average.

So we shorted the S&P 500 on this day at its closing price of 1484.50.

On 23 June 2009, the 50-day moving average moved back above the 200-day moving average.

We covered our short on this day at 895.10.

This trade captured 589.40 points on the S&P 500.

At $50 per point, that comes out to a profit of $29,470 per futures contract.

If you traded 10 contracts, you made $294,700.

In order to make this money, you didn't need to know anything about the housing crisis, subprime mortgages, LIBOR, MBS, CDOs, TARP, or credit default swaps.

You just needed to trade with the trend.

This is my favorite way to profit from a bear market.

The strategy is simple, clean, and has worked quite well in the last two bear markets.

Just remember that trading futures is risky business.

It's an advanced strategy.

If you do decide to do it, remember to leave yourself some wiggle room.

Assume that the trade might go against you 1-2% before it begins to make money.

That means you'll need to have an extra two to three thousand dollars in your account per futures contract traded in order to avoid margin calls.

In the next chapter, we'll talk about another way to profit from a bear market.

FOUR

AN AUTOMATED TRADING STRATEGY THAT MAKES BIG MONEY IN A BEAR MARKET

Bull markets are characterized by low volatility.

In a bull market, the market wiggles around less and daily trading ranges are smaller.

Bear markets are characterized by high volatility.

In a bear market, daily trading ranges are higher.

You can have huge intraday swings, with the Dow being down hundreds of points one day.

And then up hundreds of points the next day.

One way to profit from a bear market is to trade a system that does well in high volatility regimes.

Intra-week mean-reversion trading strategies work well for this.

A common pattern in the stock market is a sell-off early in the week, which is followed by a mid-week recovery.

Weekends provide traders with lots of time to get nervous about their positions or about the economy.

They read the latest edition of Barron's and get spooked.

Monday morning moods are never good.

In fact, it's the most common time for a man to have a heart-attack.

Bad moods and stress translate into sell orders in the stock market.

When the stock market opens (or even just before), everyone hits the sell button.

The market will often close sharply lower on Monday.

Then, by late Tuesday or Wednesday, everyone will realize that they over-reacted.

They will buy back their stocks, thus driving the market higher.

I've created a trading system that seeks to profit from this flaw in human nature.

What you want to do is this:

You want to buy the S&P 500 (SPY or futures) at the end of the day on Monday.

Then you want to sell it at the end of the day on Wednesday.

And you only want to do it on Mondays when there is a real panic.

I measure the degree of panic by looking at the %R indicator.

%R helps to measure whether the market is currently overbought or oversold.

When %R is below 10, it is a sign that we are experiencing panic selling.

And we know that whenever we get panic selling on a Monday, we should be buying on the close.

For %R, I like to use a lookback period of 3 days.

TradeStation allows you to "backtest" trading strategies like this, to see how they would have performed in the past.

Here's the EasyLanguage code that I use in TradeStation:

```
vars: x(0);
    x=percentR(3);
    If dayofweek(date)=1 then begin
    If x<=10 then buy this bar on close;
    end;
    If dayofweek(date)=3 then begin
    If marketposition=1 then sell this bar on close;
    end;
```

In this strategy, this is how %R is calculated:

%R=100*(highest price over the last 3 days- today's closing price)/(highest price over the last 3 days- lowest price of the last 3 days)

Let's look at annual returns for this strategy:

2017: 1.41%
2016: 4.32%
2015: 6.25%
2014: 2.68%
2013: 2.90%
2012: 0.98%
2011: 11.17%
2010: 0.53%
2009: 6.18%
2008: 31.60%
2007: 10.15%
2006: 2.17%
2005: 0.84%
2004: 0.96%
2003: 7.40%
2002: 14.72%
2001: -1.23%
2000: -0.24%

Looking at these annual returns, an obvious pattern emerges:

Most of the time, the system makes just a little (or loses just a little) money.

But then during bear market years (2002, 2008) or sharp bull market corrections (2011), when volatility is high, the system makes a lot of money.

This makes perfect sense:

During high volatility regimes, the markets will sell off more deeply on those pessimistic Mondays.

And bounce back higher on those optimistic Wednesdays.

No one can say if this trading strategy will continue to work.

But if it does, it's great system to keep trading with a part of your trading account.

It makes a little money most of the time.

And then it makes a lot of money when you need it most—when times get tough.

If you trade it using 4x leverage with futures, you might be able to make 50-120% during the next bear market.

FIVE

HOW TO TELL WHEN A BEAR MARKET IS ALMOST OVER

A bear market ends when the last bullish trader finally throws in the towel.

Up to this point, he has had a higher pain tolerance than everyone else.

But now even he has hit his limit.

He simply cannot take the pain anymore.

He logs into his brokerage account, and sells all of his positions.

Now, on the margins, there is no one left to sell.

All of the weak mutual funds and hedge funds have dumped their portfolios and closed down.

Stock brokerages have just finished liquidating positions to meet the last margin call.

There are no weak hands left.

Warren Buffett still owns stocks, but he's not selling.

The little guys have sold all of their stocks.

The smart billionaires and millionaires have scooped them up at bargain basement prices.

There has been a massive transfer of wealth.

Now it's only the strong hands left.

The tide has gone out, and the fraudsters and newbies have been left high and dry on the sand.

As the old saying goes:

_____

> "When a man with money meets a man with experience, the man with experience ends up with the money, and the other ends up with the experience."

The good news is that now you are the man/woman with experience, having read this book.

In a later chapter, I'll tell you how to buy stocks at bargain basement prices, so that you can be on the same side as the millionaires and billionaires.

There are other signs that the end of the bear market is near.

Your local athletic club or golf club will no longer have CNBC on all of the TV's.

They will all be playing ESPN or sitcoms instead.

Stocks will now be a taboo subject at cocktail parties.

You'll be better off discussing religion or politics.

All of your favorite financial publications, which were so bullish at the top, will now be predicting further stock market lows.

For example, the last bear market ended on 9 March 2009.

On that same day, "The Wall Street Journal" ran an article called "How Low Can Stocks Go?"

It predicted that the Dow Jones Industrial Average would fall from its then current level of 6,500 all the way down to 5,000.

At this point, the Dow was already down 54% from its October 2007 peak.

Rather than falling, the Dow ended the year up 19%.

These financial publications and talking heads are almost always wrong.

At the market bottom in October 2002, I remember CNBC anchorwoman Maria Bartiromo (who had been one of the chief cheerleaders in the previous bull market) getting exasperated with a guest and saying:

"Why not just short all stocks?"

Maria Bartiromo was the last bull to throw in the towel.

It is only then, when there is no one left to sell. . .

when the last bull gives up. . .

that the stock market actually bottoms.

So if the Dow or S&P 500 is down over 30% from its highs. . .

If stocks have been falling for over a year. . .

If you feel sick to your stomach whenever you hear the word "stocks". . .

If you've stopped checking your stock quotes or brokerage account. . .

If every newspaper and financial website is proclaiming only "doom and gloom". . .

It's a good sign that the bottom is very near.

It's at this point that you should start looking for the SPY 50-day moving average to cross back above the 200-day moving average.

There may be fake-outs.

For example, in late April and early May 2002, the 50-day moving average for the S&P 500 was skimming just below the 200-day moving average.

It looked like it was going to cross any day, but it didn't, and then...

The market took another nose-dive and fell an additional 27%.

So it's important to wait until the actual crossover occurs.

The 50-day moving average finally closed above the 200-day moving average on 14 May 2003.

The S&P 500 was at 939.28 on this day.

It had already rallied over 22% from a low of 768.67.

It was easy to believe that the rally was over, but it was actually just getting started.

The S&P 500 rallied consistently until late December 2007, going from 939.28 all the way up to 1576.

That's another 67% rally.

Many stocks went up 100-500% over this same period.

With all of the weak hands flushed out by the bear market, stocks were free to rally for many years.

These new bull markets are easy to trade:

Simply buy the SPY (or S&P E-mini futures, if you want to be more aggressive and use leverage) when the 50-day moving average closes above the 200-day moving average.

Exit the position when the 50-day moving average closes back below the 200-day moving average.

That's it.

Sometimes the simplest systems are best.

In the next chapter, we will discuss another bear market trading strategy that will enable you to profit from the breakdown of the previous bull market leaders.

SIX
HOW TO SHORT MOMENTUM STOCKS IN A BEAR MARKET

As we have said, every bear market begins with many stocks' 50-day moving averages crossing below their 200-day moving averages.

While we cannot predict a bear market, we can certainly protect ourselves against one.

We can do this by exiting our long positions each time that a stock's 50-day moving average crosses below its 200-day moving average.

Conservative traders should not try to profit from a bear market.

They should be content with being on the sidelines.

If you are never long a stock when its 50-day moving average is below its 200-day moving average, you can avoid getting hurt most of the time.

Long-term investors should probably also not try to time the market.

Rather than watching stock prices, they should focus on company fundamentals and dividend payouts.

Of course, if it has been 5-10 years since the last bear market, smart long-term investors may decide to let their dividends and cash pile up, rather than immediately reinvesting them.

This is sometimes called "keeping your powder dry."

Warren Buffett does something similar.

He often lets his cash pile up, and then waits for a nasty bear market to deploy it.

The next strategy that I am going to teach you should only be used by aggressive traders.

You better be young, able to handle a lot of stress, and have some money that you can afford to lose.

Aggressive traders like this can make money in a bear market by shorting momentum stocks.

Stocks that have strong momentum on the way up often have even stronger momentum on the way down.

A stock that ran from 10 to 200 over three years might come crashing back down to 10 in a matter of 12 months.

Many momentum stocks end up giving back all or most of their entire bull market advance during a bear market.

For example, in the bear market of 2000-2002, many momentum stocks declined 85-100% from their highs.

Near the end of a momentum stock's long uptrend, it will frequently be trading at a truly irrational P/E multiple.

No amount of business success or growth will ever be able to justify such a multiple.

On the way up, no one cares, because everyone is making money.

But when a stock's upward momentum begins to slow, or even reverse, investors turn once again to the stock's valuation, realize how crazy it is, and decide to sell their shares.

This selling helps to accelerate the stock's downward move.

Cisco Systems (CSCO) is a perfect example of this dynamic at work:

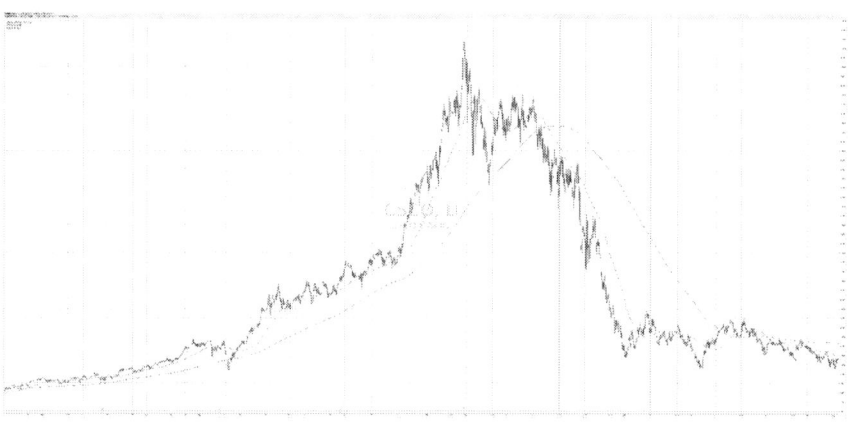

You can also access this image at the following link:
www.tradingview.com/x/jKTRuhwm/

For CSCO, the 50-day moving average crossed above the 200-day moving average on June 27, 1997 when the stock was trading at a split-adjusted price of just 7.39.

The stock proceeded to run for the next two and a half years, topping out at split-adjusted high of 82.00 and a P/E of almost 174!

The 50-day moving average finally crossed back below the 200-day moving average on October 4, 2000, at a split-adjusted closing price of 58.56.

When this happened, the stock promptly fell another 86%, finally bottoming out at split-adjusted low of 8.12 on October 8, 2002.

After a tremendous run of over 1000%, the stock retraced almost completely.

Almost everyone was surprised both by how far the stock rallied, and by how far it retraced—everyone, that is, except for the trend-followers who captured the majority of the move up and the move down.

So how does one short a momentum stock?

First, never be foolish enough to short a momentum stock until the 50-day moving average has closed below the 200-day moving average.

Many otherwise very smart traders have lost their shirts trying to short stocks like Cisco on the way up.

The stock was certainly overvalued, but it kept going up.

Second, look for stocks that have had tremendous run-ups, but whose revenue growth is beginning to slow.

The market is very quick to punish high-flying stocks whose growth begins to slow.

Shorting stocks can be quite risky, and is therefore not for everyone.

That being said, if you are able to bear the risks, the remainder of this chapter will teach you how.

To short a stock, it is first necessary for the stock to be available to "borrow" from your broker.

If you cannot find a broker who will lend you the stock from its inventory, it is impossible to short the stock.

Once you have been able to borrow shares of the stock, you sell the shares into the market ("sell short" is the broker's order that you want to use).

At the end of your trade, you will buy back the shares ("buy to cover") and deliver them back to your broker

This process of borrowing and delivery is usually automated, and is much easier than it sounds.

If the stock has declined, you will have made money. If the stock has gone up, you will have lost money.

In short selling, the key is to "sell high" and "buy low" (in that order!).

Short selling a momentum stock is further complicated by the fact that it can be tricky to figure out where to set your stop.

It is usually best to set a fairly wide stop of 10-20% (or even more) from entry.

Thus, if you short a stock at 100 and are using a 20% stop, you will exit your short if the stock trades at 120.

The problem with shorting is that your maximum profit is 100%.

For example, if you short a stock at 100 and it goes to zero, you have just made 100% (before commissions, which are minimal).

Unfortunately, you had to risk 10-20% (your stop loss) to put on this trade.

At a 20% stop, **you are basically risking 1 dollar to make 5 dollars.**

On the long-side of momentum stocks, we are often risking 15% to make 300%.

In other words, **we are risking 1 dollar to make 20 dollars.**

The risk-reward ratio of shorting is far inferior to that of going long.

For this reason, many traders will go on vacation at the beginning of a bear market.

They will have made their money in the preceding bull market, and will see no reason to endure the stress of a bear market, where the risks far out-weigh the rewards.

To summarize, for those hardy souls who want to trade momentum stocks on the downside, there are 3 things to look for:

1. The 50-day moving average needs to close below the 200-day moving average for the stock.
2. The stock needs to have had a long run-up.
3. And preferably, the stock needs to show signs of slowing growth in revenue or earnings.

In the latter category, a stock will often have an earnings miss and gap down sharply when it reports slowing growth, or revenues or earnings that are below the market's expectations.

A textbook example of a successful short is the shoemaker Crocs (CROX) in late 2007. The stock had had a long run-up, from its IPO in February 2006, all the way to October 31, 2007.

On that day, after the market closed, Crocs reported disappointing earnings and projected 2008 revenue growth that fell short of the market's expectations.

How do we know that the earnings report fell short of Wall Street's high expectations, even if we don't know how to read an earnings transcript?

Simply based on the stock's reaction: it fell in the after-hours market and closed down 36% the following day.

You can also access the chart at the following link:
www.tradingview.com/x/NMm9yLS5/

Now most people would find it quite difficult to short a stock that had already fallen 36%.

But we know that the time to short a momentum stock is when its momentum has sharply reversed, and not a moment before.

Then on January 2, 2008, the 50-day moving average closed below the 200-day moving average and the stock closed at 37.90.

If you had gone short the following day at the market open at 38.00 and set your stop at 10%, you would have been able to ride the stock all the way down from 38.00 to 3.02.

That is where the stock was trading when the 50-day moving average finally crossed back above the 200-day moving average).

You made 92% on this trade, and risked only 10%.

That is about as good as shorting can get.

There is one more thing that you should know about shorting momentum stocks.

When you borrow shares of a stock from your broker that you wish to short, you will need to pay a fee that is based on how long you borrow the shares for.

When many people are trying to short a certain stock, that stock will be on the "hard-to-borrow list"—meaning that it can be expensive to borrow the shares from a broker.

Sometimes these fees can be as high as 100% annualized.

This means that if the stock that you have shorted goes to zero in one year, you make 100%, but need to pay your broker 100% (because the stock was hard-to-borrow and you held it for 1 year at an annualized 100% borrow rate).

High borrowing costs make it extremely important to time your entry correctly (using the 50/200 moving average crossover method that we have discussed).

As we have seen, the stock needs to fall faster than your borrow rate, or you will end up losing money even if the trade itself makes money.

For example, if you have borrowed the stock at a 100% annualized borrow rate, and it falls 50% in 3 months, you are still OK.

You make 50% on the stock short, and only have to pay 25% in borrowing costs (100%/12 months times 3 months= 25%), for a net return of 50% - 25% = 25%.

Even worse, when you are short a stock, it is possible for the broker to ask for the shares back at any time.

If this occurs (and it almost always occurs at the worst possible time), you will need to cover your short (buy back the shares in the open market) wherever it happens to be trading on that day.

When shorts are forced to cover by their brokers, a stock will typically rally significantly, so that you will probably be buying back your shares at a loss.

That's the nice thing about trading S&P 500 E-mini futures instead.

It's easier to stay short, because (as long as you have met the maintenance and initial margin) your broker will never force you to cover your short.

SEVEN
WHAT STOCKS TO BUY WHEN EVERYONE ELSE IS SELLING

Near the end of a bear market, there are often many undervalued stocks available.

Investors and traders have been dumping stocks for many months.

Often they must sell stocks, even when they don't want to.

When a hedge fund or mutual fund manager gets a redemption request, he must sell stocks to raise cash.

Even if he thinks the stocks are undervalued, he must still sell them in order to return cash to his investors.

This kind of indiscriminate selling pressure will cause many stocks to trade for less than they are intrinsically worth.

Just as indiscriminate buying pressure (in the late stages of a bull market) will often cause many stocks to trade for much more than they are worth.

Value investing is simply the strategy of purchasing a stock when it is undervalued.

This can be hard to do in a bull market.

But it is relatively easy to do in a bear market.

A value investor will compare a company's normalized earnings to its current market value, to determine if a stock is undervalued.

Warren Buffett is a master of this technique.

For example, in the middle of the 2008 financial crisis, Buffett wrote:

"A simple rule dictates my buying: be fearful when others are greedy, and be greedy when others are fearful."

---

and

> "Bad news is an investor's best friend. It lets you buy a slice of America's future at a marked-down price."

The easiest time to buy a great business at a great price is during a bear market.

Let me give you an example.

In 2008, Coca-Cola (ticker KO) had earnings per share (EPS) of $1.51.

In 2009, Coke traded as low as 18.70, on a split-adjusted basis.

At that price, Coke had a trailing P/E (price to earnings ratio) of just 12.38, an earnings yield (1 divided by the P/e) of 8.08%, and a dividend yield of 4.39%.

By comparison, today (19 January 2018) Coke has a trailing P/E of 24.50, an earnings yield of 4.08%, and a dividend yield of 3.40%.

The stock has more than doubled from its lows, all while paying a healthy dividend every year.

Anyone could have bought Coke below $20 in 2009, but very few did.

It did not require inside information, or stock tips.

All that it required was nerves of steel to buy when it appeared that the financial world was ending.

How long into a bear market should one wait to buy a great business?

One method is just to wait for the dividend yield to get to 4%, or the trailing P/E (calculated using the company's last 12 months of earnings) to get to 15 or lower on a stock like Coke.

That is the "valuation method."

The second method is the "market timing" method.

It involves waiting a fixed period of time into a bear market before buying-- or waiting for a large peak to trough draw down in price.

For example, Coke peaked at 44.47 (split-adjusted) in July 1998.

It fell until March 2003, trading as low as 18.50. In other words, it fell roughly 58% from peak to trough.

Again, Coke peaked at 32.79 in January 2008, before the financial crisis really got started.

It fell until March 2009, trading as low as 18.72.

In other words, it fell roughly 43% from peak to trough.

Using this "market timing" method, you would wait for Coke to sell off 40-50% from its last highest price, and then buy your position.

Since Coke is a blue-chip stock that is included in indices like the Dow Jones Industrial Average and the S&P 500, it tends to bottom at the same time that the general stock market bottoms.

The 2000-2002 bear market lasted roughly 2 years and 7 months.

The 2008-2009 bear market lasted roughly 1 year and 4 months.

Let's say that the stock market peaks and then falls for more than 1 year.

Further, there is plenty of pessimism on TV, in the newspapers and on the internet, and all of your friends are selling their stocks.

That is the time that you want to be loading up on businesses like Coke, especially if they have fallen over 40% from their peaks, have P/E's of 15 or less, and have dividend yields approaching or exceeding 4%.

A time like this will come again.

I do not know if it will happen in 2018 or 2019, but it is certain to come.

The current bull market has been running since March 2009.

We are well overdue for a bear market.

When it comes, it is going to be brutal.

The good news is that you are now prepared.

History does not repeat, but it does rhyme.

To paraphrase Leo Tolstoy:

BEAR MARKET TRADING STRATEGIES

> "All bull markets are happy in the same way. Every bear market is unhappy in its own way."

The next bear market is going to be different (on the surface) from previous bear markets.

It should, however, roughly track the road map that I have laid out for you.

Follow the road map, instead of your emotions.

You will emerge on the other side, both wealthier and wiser.

In the meantime, I'm here to help.

If you have questions, or just want to say hi, write to me at matt@trader.university

I love to hear from my readers, and I try to answer every email personally.

I am currently getting a huge volume of email, so please keep bugging me if you don't hear back right away.

I would like to connect personally with each of you, and see if I can help you in any way.

Thanks for purchasing this book and reading it all the way to the end.

If you enjoyed this book and found it useful, I'd be very grateful if you'd post an honest review on Amazon.

Just go to www.trader.university and click the menu tab that says "Books."

Then click the book that you want to review.

Then click the blue link next to the yellow stars that says "customer reviews."

You'll then see a gray button that says "Write a customer review"—click that and you're good to go.

If you would like to learn more ways to make money in the markets, check out my other Kindle books on the next page.

ALSO BY MATTHEW R. KRATTER

Click here to buy this book on Amazon

Or simply go to www.trader.university and click on the "Books" tab.

Click here to buy this book on Amazon

Or simply go to www.trader.university and click on the "Books" tab.

YOUR FREE GIFT

Thanks for buying my book!

As a way of showing my appreciation, I've created a **Free Video Tutorial** for you.

In this video, I am going to show you some of the tools and charts that I use in my trading.

I will also give you an exact copy of the trading chart that I use to track bull and bear markets.

There was no way to include this material in a written book, so I have created this free video tutorial for you instead.

>>>Tap Here to Get the Free Video Tutorial and Charts<<<

Or simply go to:

http://www.trader.university/bear-market

ABOUT THE AUTHOR

Hi there!

My name is Matthew Kratter.

I am the founder of Trader University, and the best-selling author of multiple books on trading and investing.

I have more than 20 years of trading experience, including working at multiple hedge funds.

Most individual traders and investors are at a huge disadvantage when it comes to the markets.

Most are unable to invest in hedge funds.

Yet, when they trade their own money, they are competing against computer algorithms, math PhD's, and multi-billion dollar hedge funds.

I've been on the inside of many hedge funds.

I know how professional traders and investors think and approach the markets.

And I am committed to sharing their trading strategies with you in my books and courses.

When I am not trading or writing new books, I enjoy skiing, hiking, and otherwise hanging out in the Rocky Mountains with my wife, kids, and dogs.

If you enjoyed this book, you may also enjoy my other Kindle titles, which are available here:

http://www.trader.university

Just click on the tab that says "Books."

Or send me an email at matt@trader.university.

I would love to hear from you.

DISCLAIMER

While the author has used his best efforts in preparing this book, he makes no representations or warranties with respect to the accuracy or completeness of the contents of this book and specifically disclaims any implied warranties or merchantability or fitness for a particular purpose. The advice and strategies contained herein may not be suitable for your situation.

You should consult with a legal, financial, tax, or other professional where appropriate. Neither the publisher nor the author shall be liable for any loss of profit or any other commercial damages, including but not limited to special, incidental, consequential, or other damages.

This book is for educational purposes only. The views expressed are those of the author alone, and should not be taken as expert instruction or commands. The reader is responsible for his or her own actions.

Adherence to all applicable laws and regulations, including

72 DISCLAIMER

international, federal, state, and local laws, is the sole responsibility of the purchaser or reader.

Neither the author nor the publisher assumes any responsibility or liability whatsoever on the behalf of the purchaser or reader of these materials.

Any perceived slight of any individual or organization is purely unintentional.

Past performance is not necessarily indicative of future performance.

Forex, futures, stock, and options trading is not appropriate for everyone.

There is a substantial risk of loss associated with trading these markets. Losses can and will occur.

No system or methodology has ever been developed that can guarantee profits or ensure freedom from losses. Nor will it likely ever be.

No representation or implication is being made that using the methodologies or systems or the information contained within this book will generate profits or ensure freedom from losses.

The information contained in this book is for educational purposes only and should NOT be taken as investment advice. Examples presented here are not solicitations to buy or sell. The author, publisher, and

all affiliates assume no responsibility for your trading results.

There is a high risk in trading.

HYPOTHETICAL OR SIMULATED PERFORMANCE RESULTS HAVE CERTAIN LIMITATIONS.

UNLIKE AN ACTUAL PERFORMANCE RECORD, SIMULATED RESULTS DO NOT REPRESENT ACTUAL TRADING. ALSO, SINCE THE TRADES HAVE NOT BEEN EXECUTED, THE RESULTS MAY HAVE UNDER-OR-OVER COMPENSATED FOR THE IMPACT, IF ANY, OF CERTAIN MARKET FACTORS, SUCH AS THE LACK OF LIQUIDITY.

SIMULATED TRADING PROGRAMS IN GENERAL ARE ALSO SUBJECT TO THE FACT THAT THEY ARE DESIGNED WITH THE BENEFIT OF HINDSIGHT. NO REPRESENTATION IS BEING MADE THAT ANY ACCOUNT WILL OR IS LIKELY TO ACHIEVE PROFIT OR LOSSES SIMILAR TO THOSE SHOWN.

Made in the USA
Middletown, DE
06 September 2018